Modern Odyssey:

Poems by Dorothy Sutton

Old Seventy Creek Press 2016

OLD SEVENTY CREEK PRESS

COPYRIGHT 2016 BY Dorothy Sutton
2016 OLD SEVENTY CREEK FIRST EDITION

PRINTED IN THE UNITED STATES OF AMERICA
ALL RIGHTS RESERVED UNDER INTERNATIONAL
AND PAN-AMERICAN COPYRIGHT CONVENTIONS

PUBLISHED IN THE UNITED STATES
BY OLD SEVENTY CREEK PRESS
RUDY THOMAS, PUBLISHER
P. O. BOX 204
ALBANY, KENTUCKY 42602

ISBN-13: 978-0692620434
ISBN-10: 0692620435

For my husband Bill;

our daughters Marybeth Wallace and Sandy Larmore
and their husbands McLain and Rob; and

our grandchildren
Catherine, Elizabeth, Robert, Sutton, and Preston

ACKNOWLEDGMENTS

The author gratefully acknowledges publication in the following books and journals:

Atlanta Review: Irish Issue................"Somebody's Ashes"

Grolier Prize Poems 1991 (Boston)............ "Translations" (Winner of the 1991 Grolier Poetry Prize)

HMS Beagle: *BioMedNet Magazine* (London based) "What We Learn In Medical School"

Poetry* *(*See next page) . . . . "Darwin's Scope"

Poetry Ireland Review (Dublin)............"Haiku Love Songs" (as "First Electronic Haiku)

Prairie Schooner....................... "Deductive Reasoning"

Millennium Anthology (Morehead U. Press, 2000), rpt. *Backing Into Mountains* (Wind Publications, 2009)....... "Relatively Speaking"

Virginia Quarterly Review............... "Mother's Day Visit to the Pietà" Subsequently chosen for *Anthology of American Poetry*, (Monitor Books, 1997)

World... "Puzzle" and "What You Need to Celebrate"

Writing Who We Are Anthology (Western Kentucky University Press, 1999)......"Standing By Ourselves"

ACKNOWLEDGMENT NOTES:

*"Darwin's Scope" was first printed in *Poetry* 174.6 (September, 1999), rpt. here by kind permission of the Modern Poetry Association, Chicago; rpt. Norton Critical Edition, *Darwin*, 3rd edition, ed. Philip Appleman. New York: W. W. Norton (2001).

Some of the Darwin and Matisse poems, section III, greatly altered, first appeared in *Startling Art* (Finishing Line Press:1999), nominated for Pushcart Prize. (no longer in print)

"Somebody's Ashes" was chosen for *Best of Atlanta Review: 10th Anniversary Issue* (2005).

"A Brief History of Laughter" first appeared in *Backing Into Mountains*, 2009.

I am grateful to both Irish Arts Councils and Virginia Center for the Creative Arts for the 1995 Tyrone Guthrie Award, subsidizing my month's poetry residency at the Tyrone Guthrie International Arts Centre at Annamakerrig, County Monaghan.

I am also indebted to Bread Loaf Writers' Conference for the Robert Frost Scholarship in Poetry; to the Atlantic Center for the Arts (one of 12 nationwide chosen by James Dickey); to the Kentucky Arts Council for an 1999 Individual Artist Award in Poetry; to the Kentucky Foundation for Women for two generous grants; and to Eastern Kentucky University for sabbaticals, all of which helped make this book possible.

TABLE OF CONTENTS

I. RELATIVELY SPEAKING

Page 9 We Come In From the Stars
Page 10 Puzzle
Page 11 How Long Is the Coast Of Maine
Page 12 Human Race
Page 14 Are We More Nothing Than Something
Page 15 The Role Of Cold Dark Matter In the Birth Of the Universe
Page 16 What We Learn In Medical School
Page 17 Deductive Reasoning
Page 18 Crash
Page 19 Word Hurt
Page 20 When Your Mother Dies
Page 22 Mother's Day Visit To the Pietà
Page 23 Relatively Speaking

II. WHAT WE NEED TO CELEBRATE

Page 26 A Brief History of Laughter
Page 27 Haiku
Page 28 Haiku Love Songs
Page 29 Standing By Ourselves
Page 30 Wild Ones
Page 31 Windows
Page 32 Human Instruments
Page 33 Who Put the Pale In Palestine
Page 34 Blinders Fooling the Mule
Page 35 What You Need To Celebrate
Page 36 World Cup
Page 38 Thelonious Monk In Rocky Mount
Page 39 Transients
Page 40 Translations
Page 41 Somebody's Ashes
Page 42 Has Been
Page 43 These My Kissing Cousin Kin

III. ARTS AND SCIENCES: FINDING DESIGNS

Page 45 You Can Be Quite Deprived
Page 46 Galileo At Home
Page 48 Natural Disasters
Page 49 Modern Odyssey
Page 50 Darwin's Scope
Page 51 In Search of Earth Somewhere
Page 52 Dialogue at Down House
Page 53 Descent of Man
Page 54 Icarus Dreams of Darwin
Page 55 Darwin Delivers the Divinity School Address
Page 56 Arts and Sciences: Finding Designs
Page 57 A Clutch of Colors in His Hand
Page 59 Brush With Color, Brush With Life
Page 60 Icarus Among the Stars
Page 61 The Bright Room
Page 63 Our Professor Lectures On DNA
Page 64 The Language of Batik
Page 65 NOTES
Page 66 ABOUT THE POET

* This symbol is used to indicate a space between stanzas of a poem whenever such spaces are lost in pagination.

I. RELATIVELY SPEAKING

WE COME IN FROM THE STARS

Life emerging from heat vents
deep beneath the sea, or
before that from a larger charge--
A sexy lark, a blast wave
from an ancient exploding star
bullet-streaking across the heavens
at more than three million miles an hour,
to startle and hurtle us forward toward
these complex matters of our past,
smashing into a pocket of gas,
heating it to a fiery glow.

These shock waves racing the universe
distributed elements that made
heavenly and earthly bodies--
the planets and us.
She birthed a nursery full of stars.
Fusion of hydrogen and helium,
heat and light, self-luminous.

The star burns, creates new elements,
enriches the gas already there
with heavier elements: nickel, copper,
zinc and lead --the raw materials
from which we're made. The iron particles
building our bridges and our blood.
Our nourishing mother, the universe:
Every atom in the human body
at one time processed by a star.

PUZZLE
for my anthropology student, Joe

        Trying to make meaning
of this our long life, fitting together
pieces of the puzzling struggle:
a tooth here, fragile fragments
of skull, kneecap, femur there,
infinite stretches of silence between.
Held with conjecture's tentative glue.

Pondering pottery shards,
ashes, stones, animal bones.
Asking how, why, what, when--
and especially *who*.

Trying to make meaning of this my brief life--
are we more than the sum of our bones?
Fumbling in the dark with recalcitrant pieces.
Scattered puzzle, battered box,
key pieces missing,
no guiding picture on the top.

HOW LONG IS THE COAST OF MAINE?

It all depends.
The coast of Maine
looks smooth and short
from the window of your plane,
traversed in an hour or two,
an orderly border
unfolding below.
But to the snail
struggling
up and down
the ins and outs
of every crevice
in every granite rock--
to the snail,
who scratches his softness
over wretched grains
of shell-fragment sand,
and in his lifetime
knows only
three large boulders
and a limb,
in his lifetime
knows only a yard or two,
to him it's something else again.

HUMAN RACE

She's more than bored with birds and bees,
her mind back in her moment of triumph,
a champion in the Eighth Grade Races this morning,
still glorying in her run through the clover. How
to deal with this business, anyway--
fertilizing eggs--to a thirteen year old.

How at the bang from the starter's gun,
The runners are off--some defective
from the start, all cringing before
the many enemies.
First barricade hurdle: an acid defense
to mow down a quarter of this gang
from the other side of town. The rest
receive a testy message: 48 hours--
at most--and then you're history.

This egg hunt leads to the uptown tubes,
only one of which holds the egg-of-the-month,
two ovaries like two fists held out:
enny, meeny, miney, mo . . . .

Some weary from fighting their way upstream,
yet when they get there, nobody home.
Some swim in circles, some turn around,
head back to where they started from.
Millions of runners starting, reduced to fifty now.

The first to penetrate the egg
is the only one allowed. HOME FREE
the winner cries, breaking the ribbon,
parades around with the trophy held high
to the crowd. The rest, out of luck.
Not even a free T-shirt.

*

She's alert to hear that someone has won a prize.
We marvel together at the staggering odds
Of that particular egg being fertilized,
without which she wouldn't have been herself,
but a musician? A magician? A math whiz instead?
One who fell by the side? Perplexed
with wonder, we ponder that so many
of our long line of family
were conceived at all,
in that struggling warm-up
for the race that was yet to come.

ARE WE MORE NOTHING THAN SOMETHING

as the experts insist? No more than
endless acres of wasted space
filling up each molecule, as would
two basketballs on a football field?

Some close their airports to nothing but local
to thwart this theme which seems to be chaos,
stunning runways in all directions.
I subscribe to a second opinion:
I need to be held, the way my mother
lifted me high as I gurgled with pleasure,

beyond the singing bells of telling,
and then she held me close again.
A hug feels good, but holding bodes better,
the ocean bearable with a shore somewhere
to come back to. Like you hold me now,
causing all of my protons and neutrons
to spin into space again, then shift into place again,
all of my molecules mingling with joy.

THE ROLE OF COLD DARK MATTER
IN THE BIRTH OF THE UNIVERSE

Turn your telescope this way,
texturing the galaxies.
Invisible tatters of cold dark matter,
fluctuations, crumpled crinkles
developing from silk-sheet smoothness

that first second after the Big Bang,
explosive moment blistering skies--
some fourteen some *billion* years ago?
Everything takes longer than you think it will,
even these wrinkles on the face of time.

Matter began to accumulate
(a law of nature?) everywhere: witness
your waist, those pesky papers on your desk .
TODAY produced and directed by
that swirling early universe.

What's the matter? Cancer's the matter
gathered in my grandfather's cells.
No complaints, no fear we can see.
We untangle his sheets, stretch them taut
as old tough skin over gaunt cheekbones,

but every day: *Oh, would you mind?*
A wrinkle here that's bothering me.

Scientists at MIT and Princeton
begin to untangle, a spokesperson said,
the evolution of the cosmos,
to account for the spark that ignited the stars,
but they're not expected--not anytime soon--
to unfold the role of cold dark matter
in the birth of the universe.

WHAT WE LEARN IN MEDICAL SCHOOL

Given this unique gift
from which we unzip the jacket of flesh,
peel away with reverent care,
lift the lid and peer inside,
reach down through layer after layer of tissue,
uncover surprises hidden there.
We tune in to the interplay

between the organs of the body
bribing each other into staying alive,
how blood is rushed to the vital
parts, how vulnerable our structure--
the way the delicate bones are laid,
how muscles join forces to maintain the range
of motions in the joints and limbs.

How our insides lubricate, bathe themselves
in complex juices sluicing through
sophisticated, self-cleaning machines,
interconnecting webs of mystery.
Brilliant success of flesh and bone
we never even noticed before,
this knowledge filtering through our brains
on its way to our healing hands.

Since 2001, "What We Learn In Medical School" has been distributed to students in cadaver classes, University of Manitoba Medical School, Winnipeg; and also read at the end of each year at the burial ceremony of appreciation for the donation of bodies to the medical school.

DEDUCTIVE REASONING

His filament must be attached somewhere
To range like that in the dangerous air

I cannot think down from the top
Only from the bottom up

Even home is a relative term
Atonal music has no home

Generally speaking, we believe
In whatever linen we can weave

It's the slubs that rub our psyches rough
Like what to do with the rest of our lives

And who do we want to spend it with
And how can we hang out under a bomb

With no filament to dangle from.

CRASH

I marched in the procession of grief,
graduating with full honors,
my long, black robe covering

any colors hidden beneath. Someone lifted
over my head and around my neck
a velvet hood weighed down in back

with bars of iron and stacks of wood.
My mouth a Sahara. I can't begin
to tell you why all the moisture was gone.

Breathing with open mouth? But that's impossible--
most of the time I would forget
to breathe at all, until in a moment

of panic I'd remember, take
a greedy gulp and almost choke and then--
almost as soon again forget.

Surely reading and writing would save me
as it always had before,
but concentration took the train

over a vast Arctic region.
I couldn't write anything *with* you in it,
couldn't write anything *without* you in it,

couldn't read at all. The black lines
of little cars not parallel.
They kept jumping their tracks and crashing,

rolling down the ravine in flames,
and at the end, I couldn't even
remember what their freight had been.

WORD HURT

Your words are rough.
They hurt my ear.
You love me as much
as that cricket there,
the fricatives of
his brittle legs clicking
Against the hot night air.

WHEN YOUR MOTHER DIES

*When an elder in the tribe dies,
it's like a library burning down.*
But the flames continue to climb:
museum, marketplace, the church,
courthouse, town hall. Well gone dry.
Airport, bus terminal, train station
closed for good.

Why do we write and tell our stories?
According to Rachel, the guards in the camps
delighted in telling the inmates there
their stories would never be known to the world,
their suffering would die with them.
This prospect of oblivion
added to the torturing.

Why do we write?
Because we know
that history is that part of the past
that somehow manages to escape.
But in order for this to happen,
someone must stand and testify.
Someone must say: *Yes, I remember.
This is the way things were back then*.

An elder like your mother dies,
what she could say imprisoned for life.
What she knew of her grandmother's time
and place of birth, her own mother's dream,
what caused her greatest joy and pain.

*

No one to tell you what she did
to food to make it taste so good:
the ultimate knowledge of a summer squash.
The feelings in her deepest heart.
Your history takes a tilt towards chaos,
erased of the page where she'd written her name.

The first quotation of this poem is from an old folk saying.

MOTHER'S DAY VISIT TO THE PIETÀ

Divinity has nothing to do with it,
this matter of simple arithmetic:
Even if she was just an unruffled seventeen
when he was born, she would be
a frazzled fifty when he died at thirty-three.

So why do they sculpt and paint her
as a young, innocent Italian girl
instead of a battle-scarred Jewish mother
whose child gave her no end of trouble,
constantly breaking her heart and all the rules.

She knew he was headed for an unhappy end,
every night the possibility
of some disembodied voice
from some important, impersonal place
like the police station or the morgue

belaboring the disgrace he had brought
upon family and friends. A woman sculptor
or painter would have included the wrinkles,
the pounds she gained as garbage disposal
for his lunch box after school, her rat's nest

of uncombed hair this morning, already late
on her way to make arrangements for the tomb.
And then there was all that ungodly lightning
and thunder and earthquakes and rain
she slogged through to get here.

A mother would have sculpted in the pain.

RELATIVELY SPEAKING

I.

Too many relatives in her life.
Can't shake a tree without a cousin falling out.
There in Kentucky, when she tells her name,
the response she receives is always the same:
You any kin to such and such?

Relative tuning for her dulcimer
shuns external authority.
Alone in a field or forest glen,
she can still be in harmony.
The first string can be anything:
the others adjust to be in tune.

Ptolemy saw her as Select,
center of the universe,
God as Pitch Pipe, calling the songs.
Galileo's telescope
poked her from her central place
to float about somewhere in space.

Eighteen centuries, positive of God,
HIS WILL inscribed in Black and White.
Then Darwin evolved, noticed us kin
to the animal world--and to everyone
on the planet earth, (a new Great Chain
of Being us). He helped her puncture
piñata platitudes,
leaving the husk to swing from the tree,
her blindfold removed
to new possibilities:
Character--Hard work--Luck--*Mutation*
made her what she is today?
Nature selected who she'd be?

*

II.

At first this playground frightened her,
holding onto Einstein's waist,
sliding with the speed of light
down the curves of time and space.
Quarks and quasars, quantum leaps.
Down from the monkey bars she climbs,
then teeter-totters between
up in the air and solid ground.
Towards a larger sky she swings.
She holds on tight to the whirl-around,
centers herself from its dizzying spin:

Earth embodiment of the stars,
her body the elements of the earth,
her relation to animals, earth, and stars.
She plucks her dulcimer and sings
her links with this new, inclusive kin.
No longer afraid of relatives,
she opens her door to welcome them.

II. WHAT WE NEED TO CELEBRATE

A BRIEF HISTORY OF LAUGHTER

In ancient Greece, an effective weapon
to rend political enemies.
In the Middle Ages considered frivolous
in this world bowed down, a vale of tears,
this struggle towards the next world of light.

In the eighteenth century, only deviants
and derelicts free to laugh freely,
or so it was claimed--but wait!
Serious people may hold back their laughter,
but who's that refusing to ask permission?

In the kitchen and out in the garden,
laughter splashing from the streams:
the titter of women doing laundry, the
giggles and sniggers of children. Raucous,
cackling explosions, the guffaws of the field hands.

I confess to illicit laughter,
peasant woman that I am,
so little to spare for medical fees.
Laughter that tickles and juggles my guts--
is always available, a drug that's free,

that doesn't need an expensive prescription
bearing a fancy doctor's name.
Laughter sooths my need to say myself,
to be myself, a vent for my feelings,
a pressure valve to let off steam.

HAIKU

Sun behind the clouds
I will woo him with my words
Win him back again.

Question mark the hook
You fish answers from the dark
Drag them to the light.

Orange marigold
Tiger lily, robin breast
Spring repeats itself.

You were mean to me
I'll be sad another time
Strawberries are ripe.

HAIKU LOVE SONGS

Pencil lead cuts harsh
Words of love need gentle brush
Japanese caress.

Smudged computer screen
Trace of oil from fingertip
Where I touched your name.

STANDING BY OURSELVES
Stonemason's daughter

Sadly she muses: we're each alone,
marriage the least of remedies.
No one can understand her unique self,
not being born the exact same time,
the exact same place as she was born.

And did she matter to the gods she feared
might have been shattered on Galapagos
in a finch's beak? Crushed beyond belief
beneath the rocks of ages, smashed
by extended lens of microscope and telescope?

She works the rock fence, drifts into a mantra:
never alone if she stands by herself,
if she matters to herself--
and possibly some day to another
someone who may respect, admire,
approve, appreciate the way
she's learned to lay stone upon stone.

WILD ONES

Words drip from the faucets,
mutter and chatter and sputter
with the onions over the fire,
sleep in heaps on the warm
hand of sunlight clutching the rug,
docile and oh-so-domestic then.

The trouble comes when they begin
to stamp their tiny, insolent feet,
shed their outgrown pj's,
pull thin black lives on over their heads,
strike out on their own,
feral, allergic to rules,
jump on waiting motorcycles,
ride off into the storm.

WINDOWS

What does this window mean?

It means to answer its own needs.

But what does it need?

To be conceived,
to be constructed, crafted with care
so it will work to do all the things
it was meant to do. To attract you to it.
It needs to be seen, to be seen *through*
to the changing, expansive world out there.
(Each time you look, you see things
You've never seen before.)
It needs to be sometimes blurred with jam
left over from wandering baby hands.
It needs to be used. It needs to be clear.
To be cleaned every now and again
(though even bird splats are interesting).
But don't clean frost crystals. Let them remain.

Does it need to be broken?
How else could it know
what it's like to be shattered?
Then it needs repair, to close
that hole so winter can't come in.
It needs to go both up and down
and to hover somewhere in between.
It needs about equal light and dark,
and if you've got it to spare,
maybe a little of everything?

HUMAN INSTRUMENTS
for Ludwig Van Beethoven

Composers who followed, notably Mahler,
added voice to symphony.
But before you, no one had.
The isolation of your deaf--silent world,
long custody battle for nephew Karl,
Karl's attempted suicide.
Profoundly depressed, suicidal yourself,
this lowest point in your life, you composed
the most remarkable pouring forth
of joy the world had ever known.

Critics wondered if you were losing your mind:
human voices where they'd never been.
Shouldn't you have to justify
 this raging break with an earlier age,
this bending conventions of the time?

Did you begin with instruments, just could not
say what you wanted to say
except through the human, added to strings
and wood and brass? You just decided
to do it that way? You never explained.

Silence followed that first performance,
and then they turned you around to see
hundreds of human instruments,
applauding odes of joy in your name.

WHO PUT THE PALE IN PALESTINE?

Your fat history richer than my own
bare-bone, flint-edged, protestant one,
icy as the North Atlantic
we floundered across to reach these shores,
gray and strait-laced, hard and unyielding
as the Plymouth Rock we founded it on.

We envied you the laughter, dancing,
singing, drinking, anything really
you wanted to do. Because you
could always confess and be absolved

while we labored under a cloud of guilt,
a god of thunder, afraid to die,
never certain that we were saved.
Because we had only God's word,
and the preacher's word, and our own word
that such a grace had taken place--
and we'd been sometimes known to lie.

BLINDERS FOOLING THE MULE

Emerging from the service at church,
out of darkness, sudden light
hurting me into need for dark glasses,
like blinders used to fool the mule,
protection from a beckoning world,

distraction from the task at hand.
So he wouldn't learn to love the treasures:
see the corn and hunger to grind it
between his teeth to drip in puddles
lulling his gullet, sweet, and warm.

Wouldn't thirst for the flippant stream
crawling the border of our farm,
wouldn't stop his work to mark
the crisp red fling of a cardinal's wing,
the bristled quills of forsythia.

Blinders that closed him off from vexation
of sex, protecting from the rash
temptation to throw off his harness,
to run with madness through the pasture,
worshipping the sun.

WHAT YOU NEED TO CELEBRATE

To celebrate this Holy Day,
first you need hunger.
Then you need someone
who took the trouble
to cook special food--
someone you love,
even if that someone is you.

To celebrate this Sacred Night,
first you need thirst,
and something to drink
that will make you dizzy:
that will help you remember,
that will let you forget.

Then you need darkness
to serve as a backdrop
for the candles you light.

WORLD CUP
for poet and soccer lover David Citino, battling MS

Dancing Brazilians, singing Italians,
the chants to the beat of samba drums:
Forza Italia! Flags red, white, and green,
bells ringing, *Olé, Bra-zeeel, Bra-zeeel.*
Swiveling hips of truth in moving.
No one mounts an attack like Brazil:
down the middle searing runs.

You're partial of course to Italy,
your fellow countrymen's intensity
and immaculate skill, their passion matched only
by the disturbing fervor of your words.
Remember the wounded--inflamed Achilles tendon
throbbing, strained hamstring aching.
Those who could not win, but they would play.
They cannot let this World Cup pass

any more than you can defeat
what hobbles you, gobbling your energy
to drag you down. You keep putting one
word in front of another, poem after poem.
Years of focused discipline,
dedication, concentration.
Work behind the scenes turned
to dazzling dexterity, fancy footwork,
the nimble stepping of your dance
around each awkward circumstance,
sending the ball through to its goal.
Frustration worked and cajoled into wholeness.
You poured the world into your cup,
and offered it back to the world in return.

*

Your game often halted for necessary roughness
but never called on account of dark.
Like soccer's complex mixture
of strategy, energy, ballet, chess,
with elements of the barroom brawl.

These conditions that can't be healed;
instead make you feel you've been bulldozed
by the whole Bulgarian soccer team.
Then you remember: everyone plays
the game in pain one way or another--
play with our innocent knees exposed.

*David Citino, author of a dozen books of poetry and
for many years poetry editor of The Ohio State University
Press, died of complications from multiple sclerosis at the age
of 58.*

THELONIOUS MONK IN ROCKY MOUNT

For my granddaughter, Catherine Stuart Wallace

Congratulations!
for winning your first Art Show Medal
in your North Carolina town.
Rocky Mount must be proud of you.
Thelonious Monk was born there too,
and when he was just about your age,
he felt the music coming on.

Rhythm was his first, best friend,
then harmony--to taste and savor
the holy notes as they slipped down.
He gave pleasure to everyone who heard him
smiling and tapping out his songs--
to himself too, in the bargaining.
He'd tell you it's not your award that counts,

that "*Best-of-the-Four-Year-Olds*" routine.
What's important is that for the very first time,
you've created something beautiful--
besides yourself, I mean.
The music was in there all along
to be set free by your patient hands:
You took the clay and mashed and squashed
it into a bowl, then you pressed

into its flesh the twigs of evergreen.
How does it feel--no, not for the medal--
but to be seized by the magic of Rocky Mount
that squeezed Thelonious Monk into song.
How does it feel to have brought alive
this brash thing, this sassy bowl,
giving so many people pleasure
and yourself too, in the bargaining.

TRANSIENTS

Hitching a ride with Amundsen's crew
in their struggle to reach the Pole--fourteen
hundred miles through that country
where to very breathe is pain. For what?
Magnetic center shifting every day, table
of shadows, chilled silver, crystal ice
to make the eyes blur, landscape too harsh to see.

One day, exhilaration hard to control
as a runaway dog-sled team. The next day,
muscles too tired to interrupt the bones and move
them on. Trivial ruts and vast yawning, stretching
crevasses inviting us to eternal sleep.
The milky light obscures, yet enhances,
each chance encounter with the sun.

We pitch shivering tents in the burning cold
of that hostile, chaotic waste, huddle together
while yet another blizzard's thousand outraged
screams threatens the fragile, canvas circle
of unsubstantial lantern glow. We laugh, talk,
dare to like each other, not caring if it shows,
toast each other from champagne bottles

we have slept with to keep from the cold,
melting brittle silences between.
Drinking in the latitude, the longitude--
the magnitude of our discovery. After
the blizzard, we go outside and look back
at our tent illumined by gold, by the radiant,
critical flicker of our lantern flame.

TRANSLATIONS

    Pulitzer Prize for Best Translating goes to Women

Like misplaced persons, refugees
in foreign camp, we women translated scraps
of your verbal and written phrases
that came our way. We read your signs
as your fingers spelled out Job's despair,
Shakespeare's questions, Pope's security.

We stowed away when you hoisted sail,
we too *alone--all, all alone*
on Homer's *wine-dark sea.*
Translated "God" as the gristle and bone
new-rippling in our wombs, "Heaven" as home.
Your rebuffs we suffered, your rough language
we deciphered as your search for nurture, fear
of feelings revealed. Awkwardly we stalked
through your strange language in hopes
of decoding that you cared. We mastered the art
of twisting gingerly, extracting from you,
as newborns had been from us,
the tender words you could not say,
gently wrapping them in the warm
blankets of language we needed to hear.

The italicized lines above take sentiments from
Coleridge's "The Rime of the Ancient Mariner" (*Alone,
alone--all, all alone, / Alone on a wide, wide sea, / So
lonely 'twas / That God Himself / Scarce seemed there to
be"*).

SOMEBODY'S ASHES
Sligo, Ireland

Somebody's ashes, Marie Heaney was saying,
as we walked through St. John's graveyard
from Seamus's reading, to the reception
at The Silver Swan, *they tried to toss
into the Garavogue River here.*
(We were crossing the bridge
where Yeats used to play.)

*But the wind blew so, they wouldn't settle
onto the river to drift out to sea.*

Maybe it was better that way.
That the ashes blew back onto the people
throwing them, so he could ride home again
in the pockets and creases of the clothes
of the people he loved, and there he remained
in the bands of their hats,
in the cuffs of their trousers,
walking the hills and valleys of Sligo until this day.

HAS-BEEN

Old and ugly, nobody loves you,
withered, starting to decay,
turning rancid, flaking with rust,
shuffling each day farther from grace.
Turned out of bedroom, cast out of board room
along with the rest of the trash.
Ambition which soared in your five a.m. self
now pleads for an early bed.

You can curl up in your own little den,
burrow into the compost heap,
create at last your private space
to line with silks, velvets, satins,
fluffy feathers and fine leathers
left over from by-gone days at the ball,
snuggle cozy and warm to read
your own body, your own books at last,
your own pictures on the screen,
without interruption to answer the phone.

Young Turks will ride roughshod over
your lair on their way to the Holy Wars,
not causing you any harm.
You will mistake their rumbling thunder
for the dancing of Leprechauns.

THESE MY KISSING COUSIN KIN

Open the family scrapbook to find
DNA as paradigm
shaping our place in the scheme of things,
tracing back the trail we've come,

how we're sibling to humans all over the globe,
and to all humans down through time:
Black, pale, ruddy, brown. . .
including Jesus and Attila the Hun.

First cousins: gorillas and chimps.
Second cousins: reptiles and birds,
insects, spiders, fish, and worms.
Third cousins: plants and fungi,

protozoan, bacterium.
Kissin' cousins was the term
we used for these more distant ones.
We gather around the Thanksgiving Table

Of Elements we descended from,
with this our extended family,
extending further than we'd ever dreamed.

III ARTS AND SCIENCES: FINDING DESIGNS

YOU CAN BE QUITE DEPRIVED

Before art existed,
it was something
only lovers could say.

You can be quite deprived
without realizing it. One day
a painting, a poem, a strain
of music, a sculpture comes alive
in your eye, your ear, your hand,
whispers an immeasurably sad thing
so beautifully as to almost
make you glad, talks to you
in a quiet and steady hum,
blooms into a pungent jungle
of colors and sounds,
its resonant rhythms gently,
relentlessly stalking you
through the starkest, gloomiest
corners in the cellars of your mind.

Admit it.
You were poor beyond measure
until you came into that room.

GALILEO AT HOME
1564-1642

1.

All the while he alters the old,
straddles matter and energy,
pours math into the vacuums of the princes' heads,
broadcasts the news from outer space,
re-choreographs the dance of the stars,
and pens tomes of science the commoner
could understand, he keeps on defending
his bold theories--to the Pope's chagrin.

2.

All this while, he also takes time
to buy thread for his daughter, a convent nun,
to shop for lace to grace the cuffs of his young son,
to grow oranges and lemons and rosemary leaves
for their kitchen at San Matteo,
and to cultivate grapes for their wine.

3.

This is where we are, and when:
For science at odds with the church,
Galileo's friend, Bruno, is burned.
Florentine monasteries house holy relics
including fifty-one "authentic" thorns
from Jesus's final crown: Pain as revenge
for offers of unwanted truths to humankind.

*

4.

Eighty-year-old Galileo
is summoned to the Vatican,
forced to crawl on arthritic-hinged knees,
reciting his punishment, The Penitential Psalms,
for daring to suggest the earth moved around the sun:
"Blessed is he whose transgression is forgiven. . . ."

5.

On and on he drones, till he
perceives a glow of a different kind:
(his eyes light up, he suppresses a smile)
An idea for a book--on motion--swims into his view,
moves in a long, slow orbit
around the solar brilliance of his mind.

NATURAL DISASTERS
for Charles Darwin 1809-1882

My eight-year-old heart broken, eyes overwhelmed
by the beauty, wonder, and awe of that terrible scene:
Mother laid out like that in her black velvet gown.
We children never spoke of her again.
Off to Edinburgh Medical School at sixteen,
before anesthesia; buckets of sawdust caught the blood.
I ran from surgery, the strapped-down child's screams,
echoing later through earthquakes in Concepción mud.
The sun went out with my Annie's death at ten,
the final vote of this lethal legislature
of natural disasters. The world, then,
neither moral nor just: almost as if nature
cared enough to plant the evidence there
to let me know that nature does not care.

In 2001, this sonnet was read by Richard Dawkins (then professor of evolutionary biology at Oxford University) at the ceremony inducting him into the Royal Society in London. After he signed the official book, he was allowed to look back earlier in the book to see the 19th century signature of fellow inductee Charles Darwin, whose great-great-grandson was in attendance at the ceremony.

MODERN ODYSSEY

My life work was settled then.
I would be a minister,
but first this scientific journey
to the far reaches of the earth,
going by ship, my hammock slung
over the oak chart table,
the skylight just twenty-four inches above my nose,
a drawer removed to make room for my feet.

You might ask how my six-foot frame could endure
five years in the cramped, shared space
of that *Beagle* cabin, eleven by ten,
the ceiling not even six feet high.

But I had found a blessed place,
a calling, a way to spend my time
(though often sea-sick in nauseous gloom)
devouring the thick geology books
I'd brought along. Near the skylight I was,
and could peruse earth's history
or reconstruct lectures from science class,
finding causations, connections which seemed
Divinely inspired. That was the room
I withdrew to this long, lonely while,
confined to the silent, solemn, secret,
sacred spaces of the mind.

DARWIN'S SCOPE

To get it right, he had to become an actor,
create the illusion that this event glistened
unfolding now for the first time. He had to
listen to the other actors, *listen*
to the world's voices as if he had never heard
what they said. With microscope he saw to the end
and beyond: beneath, around the secret words,
past the scope of where we'd gone before, transcended
mystery and secrets to what was more wondrous still:
the way the earth came into being, facts,
conclusions he did not want to know, revealed,
fossils from an earlier life. He packed
them up and sent them home, crate after crate,
what would become the bones of his childhood faith.

IN SEARCH OF EARTH SOMEWHERE
a sonnet for Charles Darwin 1809-1882

Not a difficult task for him to do,
this matter of planting bulbs upside down,
watching with detached, clinical certitude
as wretched root-tips twisted towards the ground
in search of earth somewhere. Not hard to deprive
the plants of sleep by tying exhausted leaves
open, observing how long it took them to die.
Easy to measure, calculate, record these
facts. While ten-year-old daughter, Annie, writhes
in his mind, dying helpless and in pain.
Feelings bloom beyond his control, shying
away from being measured or tied down,
resisting what he had trained them to do, free
of being catalogued scientifically.

DIALOGUE AT DOWN HOUSE

Darwin: I didn't want to make a fuss.
I like myself--truly--but still I have,
deep down somewhere, a need for others
to like me too. The *worst* that can be said
for people like us, I guess, is that we're willing
to make a fool of ourselves in the name of the word--
the honest word. Perhaps it's also the *best*?

Interviewer: Questioning, redefining the nature of God,
still you would not speak publicly of your belief
or violently assail another's faith.
"People believe what they must," you said.
You embraced the phases of the world with such fervor,
that, needing a warmth like that to help me hold on,
I could turn and live in your yearning glow forever.
That grace through darkness
made you large and strong,
and brave enough to face the grueling test,
bracing yourself for the stark departure
of almost every angel you had known.

*Note: The village changed its spelling to "Downe"
in mid-19th century, to avoid confusion with County Down in
Ireland. Down House (Darwin's home) retained the old
spelling.*

DESCENT OF MAN

Darwin's anguish was a mental one,
not thirty hours, but thirty years.

Towards the end of his long life,
towards the end of each long day,
his stressed mind and body, in need
of rest, shuffled from his upstairs study,
descending several times the stairs
to his new drawing room to see
if the clock ticked any faster there.

ICARUS DREAMS OF DARWIN

Nice to meet you, my gentle friend
Everyone sees you as sweet and calm
I see you more as Eve, Apollo,
Prometheus, and Poetry all rolled into one
Reaching for knowledge, the stars, the moon
The sun. Like Faust and me, the lust to explore
To experience it *all*, to know it *now*,
Awake, aware, through questioning.

Falling with me into the deep
Where sleep the wounded, weary ones
You settled in to count the waves
To tally fishes, to investigate
To estimate algae in that pond.

Sometimes you felt bound to a rock
The vulture tearing at your flesh
You marveled at his wing span
With what precision he did the job
His beak and talons evolved to do
Noted the feathers, barb, and vane.

I admire most your open mind
No, passion is your greatest trait
The way you go at it, beak and talon
No, it's your honesty
No, it's close attention to detail
You, the world's greatest lover
You greatest lover of the world.

DARWIN DELIVERS THE DIVINITY SCHOOL ADDRESS

It was all out there with Zeus or Allah
or whatever you call your *Significant Other*.
Rules and laws inscribed on the dawn
by fingers the early ones called Divine.

What, after all, is "original sin"?
"Original selfishness" a more accurate term?
Essential equipment in the human design,
the instructions free with every newborn.

Destructive predators and storms--
whether from nature or humans who lie,
cheat, and kill--those are the reasons
the helpless require legal shields.

So let's *keep* our structured world of laws!
Whoever said the laws had to go
just because some origins may be gone?
Pondering the possibility that these rules

and laws might have evolved from
our *Significant Other*,
the oh-so-magnificent Human Brain.

ARTS AND SCIENCES: FINDING DESIGNS

The art of science, the science of art
both to perceive and to mastermind
these scattered patterns we call design.
Mapping the paths we've traveled thus far
to see how they converge on this spot.
Seeing ways to say it back

in a splendid rendering of the natural world.
Heightened sensitivity,
detecting connections, solving problems,
an organ sending forth its music
to keep us in tune.

Magnifying glass, insight,
mind's eye dilated to such a point,
we see more than we've ever seen:
dappled patterns on the woodland floor
reflected in camouflage of fawn.

Poet, scientist, artist, conditioned
to observe more, expect more.
Everyday life a deep study,
developing relationships.
Lives bent towards exploration,

seeking to meet in that medium where
disparate ideas intersect
in graphic collusion. Collision--a spark.
Message of precedent, beauty of new
that had not struck our minds before.

A CLUTCH OF COLORS IN YOUR HAND
For Henri Matisse

Colors that startle, colors that shock.
It all started with a box of paints
your mother gave her little sick one
(lucky illness that would help us heal),
a clutch of colors in your hand:

I had a feeling that my life was there,
you said in awe of these newfound friends.
Once bitten by the demon Paint,
you never wanted to give it up.

First the Old Masters, then the new,
the slabs of color Cézanne laid down.
You sold your wedding ring to purchase one.

The "fauves," art's wild beasts, fast and furious,
dash on the bright, splash on the bold,
slash the canvas with crude thick lines.

You sculpted too: smoothing the bronze,
rearranging the planes of a woman's back
into geometric blocks and shapes.

I sit to feast with you, Matisse,
warm and vibrant compelling rain
telling my crops to grow,

*

You stuffed hyacinth bulbs into soil in the fall,
arming alarms to go off in the spring.
Your eyes the windows I climb through
to the other side of the dark. Then spread
out before me your trenchant work,
each unimpeachable vision of fire
recounting luminosity.
    I have a feeling that my life is here.

Italicized phrases in the Matisse poems are
sentiments attributed to the artist.

BRUSH WITH COLOR, BRUSH WITH LIFE
Le Danse II

The human race, instead of racing
against each other, try holding hands,
the flames of their exuberant flesh
enhancing the field of blue and green
with sensuous curve of extended back.

Two of them reaching, not quite touching,
dancing beyond the frame's control,
rolling right off the edge of the page.
Flouting the rules of natural perspective,
you laugh at directives to guide the race.

You try to apply for the Great War,
but your ill health serves you well,
leaves you to brush, instead of death,
another brightness, in the South of France.
The war madness finally grinding halt,

the world pensive from its vast effect,
barely surviving that surgery,
now wakes to your spiraling patterns and shapes,
your love song to the world, Matisse.
(Each day that dawns is a gift to me.)

ICARUS AMONG THE STARS

Icare

Icarus, you cut-up cutout for Jazz,
dancing as you fall through the stars,
not head-down as one would expect,
but reckless, exuberant, thighs thick
from a lifetime of dance, arms spread
for ready embrace, your heart open
for all the waltzing who fall your way.
They called you detached, undone by the sun,
but your life was there, in that atmosphere.
Such a mixture of stress and rapture,
such a juncture of earth and stars,
I have to be on guard every minute
lest I be lost to wander forever
the boundless corridors of your spirit,
the sensuous reaches of your mind.

THE BRIGHT ROOM

No paper brilliant enough for you,
you painted your own with hues so bright
the doctor prescribed you wear dark glasses
when using that room. You designed
murals, chasubles, a crucifix for
the chapel at Vence. *The essential here
is to be in a frame of mind like prayer.*

They called your chapel a work of faith,
Matisse turning at last to God.
You wouldn't concur. *My only religion
my love for the work that I have to do.
Art is the only religion I know.*
Nearing eighty did not stop you.
Out of your bed sprang new designs

from your brush attached to a bamboo pole,
from scissored pieces of colored paper
you attached to the wall. At eighty-three,
you splashed a swimming pool around

the corners of your room, huge blue
dance of dolphin-like humans
sylphing in and out of the waves,
immersed in the sea-swells of your bounty,
sounding the deeps of your mind.

*

A Blue Nude collage broken into
elbows, knees, hip, and wrist,
jagged bones of arthritic pain.
Soothed with the comforting solace of art,
we can fuse ourselves together again.

OUR PROFESSOR LECTURES ON DNA

1.

Keeper of the keys to life,
the double helix, twin spiral,
essence of the molecule.
It stores the code each cell will use
to duplicate and to sustain
humans and bees, wild flowers, and microbes.
Here lies the gentle genetic code
which urged my eyes to blue,
painted the peacock's feathers iridescent,
cracked the lilacs into perfumed bloom.

2.

A pair of pretty party streamers
wrapped in spherical embrace,
a spiral staircase we could climb
to understand what we're made from.
Strands of living tissue encrypted
with human identity. Peering into
our molecular substructure, we discover
the recipe nature used for cooking
those coded genes, descent
from a common ancestry.

3.

Our professor lectures on and on.
I glance at you. You smile at me.
The rest of the lecture I'm in a dream
of our double helixes, mine and yours,
sweetly interlocked, entwined,
in mystical harmony.

THE LANGUAGE OF BATIK

Speaking the language of batik,
She depicts the story of humankind,
Evolution's long, slow climb.

Versed in the technique of batik,
She paints with wax and dips in dye,
Over and over again.

Cannot look back to correct mistakes,
Must work with errors as best she can,
Knowing that lurking still in the fabric,
In the wondrous, final, finished product,
Some flaws remain.

END NOTES

The Darwin poems came about as a result of my reading Adrian Desmond and James Moore's exceptional biography, *Darwin: The Life of a Tormented Evolutionist*. New York: W. W. Norton, 1991. See pages 460-461 of that book for my allusion to Darwin's search for a faster clock ("Descent of Man," p. 53) that would give the exhausted man permission to retire each evening.

Two lines from "Arts and Sciences: Finding Design" (p. 56) beginning "Dappled patterns . . ." are a slight variation on lines used by permission from Richard Dawkins' poetic book of science, *Unweaving the Rainbow*.

Inspiration and information for the Matisse poems came from *Matisse* by Antony Mason. London: Aladdin Books, 1995, and from a special Matisse exhibit at the High Museum, Atlanta (on loan from Museum of Modern Art, New York). Three of the Matisse poems were based on two paintings and a collage by Henri Matisse: *Icare*, *Le Danse II*, and *The Blue Nude*.

ABOUT THE POET

Dorothy Sutton's previous books of poetry are *Backing Into Mountains* (Wind Publications, 2009) and *Startling Art* (Finishing Line Press, 1999), nominated for a Pushcart Award. Her work appears in such noted journals and anthologies as *Poetry*; *Norton Critical Edition: Darwin*; *The Hudson Review*; *Poetry Ireland Review*; *Poetry Wales*; *Southern Review*; *Antioch Review*; *Prairie Schooner*; *Virginia Quarterly Review*; and *Quadrant* (Australia), among many others. She has given scores of poetry readings across the U.S., and in Ireland.

Among residencies awarded to Sutton are such places as Virginia Center for the Creative Arts, Atlantic Center for the Arts, and Annamakerrig in Ireland. Other awards include Robert Frost Scholarship from Bread Loaf Writing Conference, the Grolier Prize, and grants from the Kentucky Arts Council. In 2010, The Carnegie Center added her to its Kentucky Great Writers list.

Professor Emerita at Eastern Kentucky University, Sutton was awarded its two highest honors, the Alumni Excellence in Teaching Award and a Foundation Professorship. She directed the annual Creative Writing Conference there for ten years. She has taught Irish literature in Dublin, Galway, and Sligo through Kentucky's Study Abroad Program. For more than twenty years, she has continued to edit poetry for an international magazine, *The Chaffin Journal*.

For more information, the poet may be reached at her website: people.eku.edu/Sutton or by email at dorothy.sutton@eku.edu

www.ingramcontent.com/pod-product-compliance
Lightning Source LLC
Chambersburg PA
CBHW072015060426
42446CB00043B/2561